THE COLLEGE COOKBOOK

DELICIOUS AND EASY COLLEGE RECIPES

By
BookSumo Press

Published by
BookSumo Press, a DBA of Saxonberg Associates
http://www.booksumo.com/

ABOUT THE AUTHOR.

BookSumo Press is a publisher of unique, easy, and healthy cookbooks.

Our cookbooks span all topics and all subjects. If you want a deep dive into the possibilities of cooking with any type of ingredient. Then BookSumo Press is your go to place for robust yet simple and delicious cookbooks and recipes. Whether you are looking for great tasting pressure cooker recipes or authentic ethic and cultural food. BookSumo Press has a delicious and easy cookbook for you.

With simple ingredients, and even simpler step-by-step instructions BookSumo cookbooks get everyone in the kitchen chefing delicious meals.

BookSumo is an independent publisher of books operating in the beautiful Garden State (NJ) and our team of chefs and kitchen experts are here to teach, eat, and be merry!

INTRODUCTION

Welcome to *The Effortless Chef Series*! Thank you for taking the time to purchase this cookbook.

Come take a journey into the delights of easy cooking. The point of this cookbook and all BookSumo Press cookbooks is to exemplify the effortless nature of cooking simply.

In this book we focus on great tasting but fairly simple college recipes. You will find that even though the recipes are simple, the taste of the dishes are quite amazing.

So will you take an adventure in simple cooking? If the answer is yes please consult the table of contents to find the dishes you are most interested in.

Once you are ready, jump right in and start cooking.

— BookSumo Press

TABLE OF CONTENTS

About the Author..2

Introduction 3

Table of Contents 4

Any Issues? Contact Us 9

Legal Notes..10

Common Abbreviations 11

Chapter 1: Easy College Recipes 12

   A Hearty Homemade Tomato Spaghetti 12

   Eggs in a Boat 15

   The Simple Frittata Formula 17

   The Quickest Mac 'n' Cheese................................20

   Simple Sriracha Chicken.......................................22

   Healthier Burritos 101 25

Advanced Ramen for College 27

Cheesy Ramen 29

Ramen Frittata 31

Quick Mozzarella Pasta Salad 33

Quick Stovetop Pasta 35

Buffalo Fries 37

Breakfast Burritos from Mexico 40

Meatball Sub 42

Sweet and Sour Ground Beef 45

Tijuana Ground Beef 47

(Mexican Style) 47

Stroganoff 50

Classical Ground Beef 53

Ground Beef Macaroni 55

How to Make Taco Filling 57

Ramen Ground Beef 59

Meat Loaf with Oats 61

Simple Cream of Meatball 63

Potatoes and Garlic 65

Baked Potatoes Remix 67

Sunbelt Classic Chicken 69

Lemons and Oregano Chicken 71

The Fluffy Sandwich 73

Oregano Mozzarella Sandwich 75

The Reuben Sandwich 78

Parmigiano-Reggiano Sandwich 81

TOMATO AND EGG STIR FRY 83

Chicken and Onions Tortillas 85

Pecos Pasta 88

Sweet Crepes 91

Cream Cheese Crepes 93

Classical College Burger I 96

Easy American Potato Salad 98

Chicken Parmigiana 101

Upstate New York Chicken 104

Corn and Beef Tacos 107

Keema 109

(Asian Inspired Ground Beef) 109

Creamy Ground Beef 112

Delicious Ground Beef and Tomatoes 114

Ground Beef Festival 116

The Easiest Beef Chili 118

Peppers and Onions Brown Rice 120

Oatmeal for Breakfast 122

Quick Egg Frittata 124

Disco Fries 126

(Fries with Mozzarella and Gravy) 126

Italian Style Eggs 129

Nutella Roll Up 131

Microwave Nutella Cake 133

A Hipster's Favorite Coffee 135

Taco Local 137

Spaghetti Taco 140

Authentic Tomato Sauce 142

A Simple Quiche For College 144

Chicken Cutlets 146

Simply Baked Broccoli 148

THANKS FOR READING! JOIN THE CLUB AND KEEP ON COOKING WITH 6 MORE COOKBOOKS.... 150

Come On 152

Let's Be Friends :) 152

Any Issues? Contact Us

If you find that something important to you is missing from this book please contact us at info@booksumo.com.

We will take your concerns into consideration when the 2nd edition of this book is published. And we will keep you updated!

— BookSumo Press

Legal Notes

COMMON ABBREVIATIONS

cup(s)	C.
tablespoon	tbsp
teaspoon	tsp
ounce	oz.
pound	lb

*All units used are standard American measurements

CHAPTER 1: EASY COLLEGE RECIPES

A HEARTY HOMEMADE TOMATO SPAGHETTI

If you are ever feeling homesick, being away in college. Do not worry. Just make sure you have these ingredients and a couple of hours and make a real delicious homemade style spaghetti. Invite some friends over and enjoy!

Ingredients

- 12 oz. spaghetti noodle
- 1 lb. lean ground beef
- 1 tsp salt
- 3/4 tsp white sugar
- 1 tsp dried oregano
- 1/4 tsp ground black pepper
- 1/8 tsp garlic powder
- 2 tbsp dried minced onion, optional
- 2 1/2 C. chopped tomatoes
- 1 1/3 (6 oz.) cans tomato paste
- 1 (4.5 oz.) can sliced mushrooms, optional

Directions

- Heat a skillet and cook the beef on medium heat till browned completely and drain off the excess fat.

- In a large pan, add the beef and the remaining ingredients except pasta and simmer, stirring occasionally for about 2 hours.
- Cook the spaghetti according to the package's directions and drain well.
- Pour the sauce over the spaghetti and serve.

Amount per serving (5 total)

Timing Information:

Preparation	15m
Cooking	2 h
Total Time	2h 15m

Nutritional Information:

Calories	557 kcal
Fat	20.3 g
Carbohydrates	65.7g
Protein	28.2 g
Cholesterol	68 mg
Sodium	1002 mg

* Percent Daily Values are based on a 2,000 calorie diet.

EGGS IN A BOAT

Eggs in a Boat is a classic breakfast or snack. Basically it's a slice of fried bread with an egg cooked directly in the center of the bread. It looks very cool when finished and tastes great.

Ingredients

- 1/2 tbsp butter
- 1 slice white bread
- 1 egg

Directions

- Coat your bread with butter on each of its sides. Then cut-out a circle in the middle of it.
- Whisk your egg in a small bowl. Set it aside.
- Get a skillet hot and for 1 min fry each side of the bread. Pour the egg into the hole and cook for 3 more mins.
- Enjoy.

Amount per serving (1 total)

Timing Information:

Preparation	Cooking	Total Time
10 m	10 m	20 m

Nutritional Information:

Calories	189 kcal
Fat	11.6 g
Carbohydrates	13g
Protein	8.3 g
Cholesterol	201 mg
Sodium	281 mg

* Percent Daily Values are based on a 2,000 calorie diet.

THE SIMPLE FRITTATA FORMULA

If you have never heard of "frittata" before. Do not worry. It is basically a fancy word for omelet. The idea is: you fry your egg with stuff in it then bake the whole thing for a few minutes to add more flavor.

Ingredients

- 2 large eggs
- salt
- fresh ground pepper
- 2 tbsps shredded cheese
- 2/3 C. vegetables
- 2 tbsps fresh herbs

Directions

- Set your oven to 350 degrees before doing anything else.
- Get a bowl, combine: herbs, cheese, and eggs.
- Coat a skillet with nonstick spray then add in your veggies.
- Cook the veggies for 1 min then add in the egg mix.
- Set the heat to low and let the bottom of the eggs set with a lid on the pan for 10 mins.

- Now place the frittata in the oven for 5 to 10 more mins until the top is set.
- Enjoy.

Servings Per Recipe: 1

Timing Information:

Preparation	5 mins
Total Time	25 mins

Nutritional Information:

Calories	239.0 kcal
Cholesterol	440.7mg
Sodium	408.4mg
Carbohydrates	3.0g
Protein	18.0g

* Percent Daily Values are based on a 2,000 calorie diet.

THE QUICKEST MAC 'N' CHEESE

Ingredients

- 1 cup macaroni
- 1/2 cup process cheese sauce
- 2 frankfurters, sliced
- 1 tsp grated Parmesan cheese
- 1 pinch dried oregano
- 4 buttery round crackers, crushed

Directions

- Set your oven at 350 degrees F.
- Cook pasta in salty boiling water for about 10 minutes until tender before draining it.
- Heat up cheese sauce in microwave for about 1 minute before baking the mixture of cooked pasta, oregano, cheese sauce, parmesan and sliced frankfurters for about 10 minutes.
- Serve.

Serving: 4

Timing Information:

Preparation	Cooking	Total Time
2 mins	13 mins	15 mins

Nutritional Information:

Calories	284 kcal
Carbohydrates	25.9 g
Cholesterol	36 mg
Fat	14.9 g
Fiber	1.5 g
Protein	10.8 g
Sodium	829 mg

* Percent Daily Values are based on a 2,000 calorie diet.

SIMPLE SRIRACHA CHICKEN

Ingredients

- 4 skinless, boneless chicken breast halves
- 1 C. French salad dressing
- 1/4 C. salsa
- 1 tsp dried thyme
- 2 tbsps sriracha

Directions

- Coat a casserole dish with nonstick spray then set your oven to 350 degrees before doing anything else.
- Place your pieces of chicken in the dish then get a bowl and combine: thyme, dressing, and salsa.
- Top your meat with the dressing mix then place covering of foil over the dish.
- Cook everything in the oven for 25 mins then take off the covering and continue to cook the meat for 20 more mins.

- When 10 mins is left coat the chicken with the sriracha and continue cooking everything for 10 more mins.
- Enjoy.

Amount per serving (4 total)

Timing Information:

Preparation	10 m
Cooking	35 m
Total Time	45 m

Nutritional Information:

Calories	421 kcal
Fat	30.8 g
Carbohydrates	11g
Protein	25.3 g
Cholesterol	67 mg
Sodium	677 mg

* Percent Daily Values are based on a 2,000 calorie diet.

HEALTHIER BURRITOS 101

Ingredients

- 1 (10 inch) flour tortilla
- 1/4 C. vegetarian refried beans
- 1 slice American cheese
- 1 pinch ground black pepper
- 1 tsp low-fat sour cream
- 1 dash hot pepper sauce

Directions

- For five mins warm your refried beans.
- Then warm your tortillas in the microwave for 30 secs.
- Layer beans into the tortilla then some sour cream then cheese, and some pepper.
- Finally add some hot sauce.
- Form everything into a burrito.
- Enjoy.

Amount per serving (1 total)

Timing Information:

Preparation	Cooking	Total Time
15 m	20 m	1 hr

Nutritional Information:

Calories	400 kcal
Fat	10 g
Carbohydrates	49.9g
Protein	15.8 g
Cholesterol	29 mg
Sodium	1075 mg

* Percent Daily Values are based on a 2,000 calorie diet.

ADVANCED RAMEN FOR COLLEGE

Ingredients

- 2 1/2 cups water
- 1 carrot, sliced
- 4 fresh mushrooms, sliced
- 1 (3 ounce) package ramen noodle pasta with flavor packet
- 1 egg, lightly beaten
- 1/4 cup milk (optional)

Directions

- Cook carrots and mushrooms in boiling water for about seven minutes before adding noodles and flavoring packets, and cooking all this for three more minutes.
- Pour egg into the mixture very slowly, while stirring continuously for thirty seconds to get the egg cooked.
- Add some milk before serving.

Serving: 1

Timing Information:

Preparation	Cooking	Total Time
5 mins	10 mins	15 mins

Nutritional Information:

Calories	500 kcal
Carbohydrates	66 g
Cholesterol	191 mg
Fat	19.2 g
Fiber	4.5 g
Protein	17.4 g
Sodium	1796 mg

* Percent Daily Values are based on a 2,000 calorie diet.

CHEESY RAMEN

Ingredients

- 2 cups water
- 1 (3 ounce) package any flavor ramen noodles
- 1 slice American cheese

Directions

- Cook ramen noodles in boiling water for about 2 minutes and drain it with a strainer before stirring in seasoning packet and cheese.
- Serve.

Serving: 1

Timing Information:

Preparation	Cooking	Total Time
5 mins		5 mins

Nutritional Information:

Calories	163 kcal
Carbohydrates	7.9 g
Cholesterol	27 mg
Fat	11.3 g
Fiber	0.4 g
Protein	7.5 g
Sodium	733 mg

* Percent Daily Values are based on a 2,000 calorie diet.

Ramen Frittata

Ingredients

- 2 (3 ounce) packages chicken flavored ramen noodles
- 6 eggs
- 2 tsps butter
- 1/2 cup shredded Cheddar cheese

Directions

- Cook your ramen noodles in boiling water for about 2 minutes and drain it with a strainer.
- Pour the eggs and the contents of the seasoning packets over the noodles before cooking everything in the butter for about seven minutes.
- Turn it over then cutting everything into four slices and brown both sides.
- Put some cheese over the top before serving.

Serving: 4

Timing Information:

Preparation	Cooking	Total Time
5 mins	15 mins	20 mins

Nutritional Information:

Calories	339 kcal
Carbohydrates	28.8 g
Cholesterol	302 mg
Fat	15.7 g
Fiber	1.2 g
Protein	20.3 g
Sodium	681 mg

* Percent Daily Values are based on a 2,000 calorie diet.

Quick Mozzarella Pasta Salad

Ingredients

- 1 (8 oz) package farfalle (bow tie) pasta
- 20 cherry tomatoes, halved
- 7 oz bocconcini (fresh mozzarella)
- 3/4 C. black olives
- 2 tbsps olive oil
- 6 fresh basil leaves
- 1 1/2 tsps fresh oregano leaves

Directions

- Boil your bow tie pasta for 12 mins in salt and water. Then drain excess liquid. Let it set to room temp.
- Get a bowl and mix: oregano, tomatoes, basil, olives, bocconcini, olive oil, and pasta.
- Enjoy at room temp. or chilled.

Servings: 4 servings

Timing Information:

Preparation	Cooking	Total Time
15 mins	15 mins	45 mins

Nutritional Information:

Calories	451 kcal
Carbohydrates	47.6 g
Cholesterol	39 mg
Fat	21.8 g
Fiber	3.7 g
Protein	17.3 g
Sodium	314 mg

* Percent Daily Values are based on a 2,000 calorie diet.

QUICK STOVETOP PASTA

Ingredients

- 1 (8 oz) package campanelle (little bells) pasta, or spaghetti
- 1/2 C. ricotta cheese
- 2 tbsps olive oil
- 1/4 onion, chopped
- 1 (6.5 oz) can tomato sauce

Directions

- Boil pasta in salt and water for 13 mins. Drain liquid and place in a bowl with ricotta, mix everything evenly.
- Get a frying pan and fry onions in olive oil for 8 mins. Combine in your: tomato sauce. Stir fry for 4 mins.
- Cover your noodles with the sauce, and let it sit for 7 mins.
- Enjoy.

Servings: 4 servings

Timing Information:

Preparation	Cooking	Total Time
10 mins	20 mins	30 mins

Nutritional Information:

Calories	328 kcal
Carbohydrates	47.4 g
Cholesterol	10 mg
Fat	10.2 g
Fiber	2.7 g
Protein	11.7 g
Sodium	284 mg

* Percent Daily Values are based on a 2,000 calorie diet.

BUFFALO FRIES

Ingredients

- cooking spray
- 4 large potatoes, sliced into wedges
- 2 tbsps olive oil, or to taste
- salt and ground black pepper to taste
- 1 C. Buffalo-style hot pepper sauce
- 1/4 C. melted butter, or to taste
- 1/4 C. ranch salad dressing, or to taste

Directions

- Coat a casserole dish with nonstick spray then set your oven to 400 degrees before doing anything else.
- Layer your potatoes into the dish and top them with some pepper, salt, and the olive oil.
- Cook the spuds in the oven for 35 mins then get a bowl and combine the melted butter and hot sauce.
- Stir the mix until it is smooth then add your potatoes to the mix.

- Stir everything to evenly coat the wedges then place the potatoes back into the dish.
- Top the potatoes with the ranch dressing.
- Enjoy.

Amount per serving (4 total)

Timing Information:

Preparation	10 m
Cooking	30 m
Total Time	40 m

Nutritional Information:

Calories	526 kcal
Fat	26.6 g
Carbohydrates	66.1g
Protein	8.1 g
Cholesterol	35 mg
Sodium	1765 mg

* Percent Daily Values are based on a 2,000 calorie diet.

BREAKFAST BURRITOS FROM MEXICO

Ingredients

- 1 lb bacon
- 10 eggs
- 1 (16 oz.) can refried beans
- 8 oz. shredded Cheddar cheese
- 10 (10 inch) flour tortillas

Directions

- Fry your bacon in a frying pan. Remove oil excess. For 30 secs warm the tortillas in the microwave.
- Get a pan to heat your refried beans. While the beans are heating cook your eggs in oil.
- Layer each tortilla with the following: 1 eggs, some cheese, 2 pieces of bacon. Shape into a burrito.
- Enjoy.

Amount per serving (10 total)

Timing Information:

Preparation	Cooking	Total Time
25 m		35 m

Nutritional Information:

Calories	638 kcal
Fat	39.1 g
Carbohydrates	44.9g
Protein	25.6 g
Cholesterol	244 mg
Sodium	1181 mg

* Percent Daily Values are based on a 2,000 calorie diet.

MEATBALL SUB

Ingredients

- 1 1/2 lbs lean ground beef
- 1/3 C. Italian seasoned bread crumbs
- 1/2 small onion, diced
- 1 tsp salt
- 1/2 C. shredded mozzarella cheese, divided
- 1 tbsp cracked black pepper
- 1 tsp garlic powder
- 1/2 C. marinara sauce
- 3 hoagie rolls, split lengthwise

Directions

- Set your oven to 350 degrees before doing anything else.
- Get a bowl, combine: 1/2 of the mozzarella, beef, garlic powder, bread crumbs, pepper, onions, and salt.
- Shape the mix into a large loaf then place it in a casserole dish.
- Cook the meat in the oven for 55 mins then let it cool for 10 mins.

- Cut the meat into slices then layer the pieces of meat on a roll.
- Top everything with the marinara then add a topping of cheese.
- Cover the sandwich with some foil and put everything in the oven for 20 more mins.
- Let the sandwich cool for 20 mins then cut each one in half.
- Enjoy.

Amount per serving (6 total)

Timing Information:

Preparation	15 m
Cooking	1 h 5 m
Total Time	1 h 40 m

Nutritional Information:

Calories	491 kcal
Fat	21.4 g
Carbohydrates	43.1g
Protein	29.3 g
Cholesterol	75 mg
Sodium	1068 mg

* Percent Daily Values are based on a 2,000 calorie diet.

SWEET AND SOUR GROUND BEEF

Ingredients

- 1 lb ground beef
- 1/4 cup yellow mustard
- 1 tbsp balsamic vinegar
- 1 tbsp minced garlic
- 1 1/2 tsps soy sauce
- 1 1/2 tsps honey
- 1 1/2 tsps paprika
- 1/8 tsp ground black pepper

Directions

- Cook beef over medium heat in a skillet for about seven minutes or until brown before adding mustard, paprika, balsamic vinegar, garlic, soy sauce, honey, and black pepper, and cooking all this for another three minutes.
- Serve.

Serving: 6

Timing Information:

Preparation	Cooking	Total Time
10 mins	5 mins	15 mins

Nutritional Information:

Calories	233 kcal
Carbohydrates	5.1 g
Cholesterol	71 mg
Fat	14.4 g
Fiber	0.9 g
Protein	20.2 g
Sodium	356 mg

* Percent Daily Values are based on a 2,000 calorie diet.

TIJUANA GROUND BEEF

(MEXICAN STYLE)

Ingredients

- 1 lb ground beef
- 1 cup salsa
- 1/2 cup water
- 1 green bell pepper, diced
- 1 bunch green onions, diced
- 1 (8 ounce) package wide egg noodles
- 1/2 cup sour cream
- 1/2 cup shredded Cheddar cheese
- 1 tomato, diced

Directions

- Cook ground beef in a skillet until brown before stirring in water and salsa, and cooking all this for 10 minutes.

- Now add onions and green pepper into the pan, and cook all this until you see that the veggies are tender before adding cooked noodles, grated cheese and sour cream.
- Cover it up until the cheese melts before sprinkling some tomatoes.
- Serve.

Serving: 4

Timing Information:

Preparation	Cooking	Total Time
10 mins	30 mins	40 mins

Nutritional Information:

Calories	732 kcal
Carbohydrates	52.1 g
Cholesterol	171 mg
Fat	43.7 g
Fiber	5.2 g
Protein	33.8 g
Sodium	592 mg

* Percent Daily Values are based on a 2,000 calorie diet.

STROGANOFF

Ingredients

- 2 lbs ground beef
- 2 onions, diced
- 1 clove garlic, minced
- 1 (4.5 ounce) can mushrooms, drained
- 2 tsps salt
- 1/4 tsp ground black pepper
- 2 cups hot water
- 6 cubes beef bouillon
- 4 tbsps tomato paste
- 1 1/2 cups water
- 4 tbsps all-purpose flour

Directions

- Cook ground beef, mushrooms, garlic and onions over medium heat until you see that onion is golden brown before adding salt and pepper.

- Now add tomato paste, a mixture of flour and water, 2 cups of hot water and bouillon cubes before turning down the heat to low and cooking all this for one full hour.
- Serve.

Serving: 6

Timing Information:

Preparation	Cooking	Total Time
15 mins	1 hr	1 hr 15 mins

Nutritional Information:

Calories	524 kcal
Carbohydrates	11.3 g
Cholesterol	129 mg
Fat	40.5 g
Fiber	1.7 g
Protein	27.6 g
Sodium	1923 mg

* Percent Daily Values are based on a 2,000 calorie diet.

CLASSICAL GROUND BEEF

Ingredients

- 1 lb lean ground beef
- 1 1/2 tbsps ketchup
- 1 tbsp prepared mustard
- 1 tbsp Worcestershire sauce
- 1 tbsp distilled white vinegar
- 1 small onion, grated
- 1/2 small green bell pepper, finely chopped

Directions

- At first you need to set a grill to medium heat and put some oil before starting anything else.
- Form patties from a mixture of ground beef, vinegar, ketchup, mustard, grated onion, Worcestershire sauce, and bell pepper very neatly.
- Cook on the preheated grill for about 4 minutes each side.
- Serve.

Serving: 4

Timing Information:

Preparation	Cooking	Total Time
10 mins	15 mins	1 hr

Nutritional Information:

Calories	252 kcal
Carbohydrates	4.5 g
Cholesterol	74 mg
Fat	15.9 g
Fiber	0.6 g
Protein	21.6 g
Sodium	215 mg

* Percent Daily Values are based on a 2,000 calorie diet.

Ground Beef Macaroni

Ingredients

- 1 1/2 lbs lean ground beef
- 1 green bell pepper, diced
- 1 onion, diced
- 2 (29 ounce) cans tomato sauce
- 1 (16 ounce) package macaroni

Directions

- Cook pasta according to the directions of package before draining it using a colander.
- Cook ground beef over medium heat until brown before adding chopped onion and cooking it for another few minutes to get them soft.
- Now add tomato sauce and green pepper before cooking it until pepper is soft.
- Pour this sauce over pasta for serving.

Serving: 6

Timing Information:

Preparation	Cooking	Total Time
30 mins	30 mins	1 hr

Nutritional Information:

Calories	570 kcal
Carbohydrates	72.9 g
Cholesterol	74 mg
Fat	15.5 g
Fiber	6.8 g
Protein	35.2 g
Sodium	1492 mg

* Percent Daily Values are based on a 2,000 calorie diet.

How to Make Taco Filling

Ingredients

- 1 lb lean ground beef
- 1 onion, diced
- 1/2 cup ketchup
- 1 package taco seasoning mix
- 2/3 cup cold water

Directions

- Cook ground beef and onion over medium heat before stirring in ketchup, cold water and taco seasoning, and cooking all this for 20 minutes at low heat.
- Serve.

Serving: 4

Timing Information:

Preparation	Cooking	Total Time
5 mins	25 mins	30 mins

Nutritional Information:

Calories	371 kcal
Carbohydrates	16.4 g
Cholesterol	85 mg
Fat	23.6 g
Fiber	0.5 g
Protein	21 g
Sodium	1060 mg

* Percent Daily Values are based on a 2,000 calorie diet.

Ramen Ground Beef

Ingredients

- 1 lb ground beef
- 1 (3 ounce) package Oriental flavored ramen noodles
- 1 (14.5 ounce) can diced tomatoes
- 1 (10 ounce) can whole kernel corn

Directions

- Cook beef over medium heat until you see that it is no longer pink before adding the flavor packet of the noodles, corn, noodles broken into pieces and tomatoes, and bring all this to boil.
- Now turn down the heat to low and cook for 10 minutes or until the noodles are tender.
- Serve.

Serving: 4

Timing Information:

Preparation	Cooking	Total Time
10 mins	10 mins	20 mins

Nutritional Information:

Calories	368 kcal
Carbohydrates	30.2 g
Cholesterol	69 mg
Fat	17.1 g
Fiber	2.7 g
Protein	23.3 g
Sodium	843 mg

* Percent Daily Values are based on a 2,000 calorie diet.

MEAT LOAF WITH OATS

Ingredients

- 1 lb ground beef
- 1 1/2 C. rolled oats
- 1 can French onion soup
- 2 eggs, beaten

Directions

- Set your oven to 375 degrees before doing anything else.
- Get a bowl, mix: beaten eggs, onion soup, oats, and beef.
- Put everything into your loaf pan.
- Bake for 1 hour and 20 mins. Ensure the internal temperature of the meat loaf 160 degrees before removing from oven.
- Enjoy.

Servings: 1 8-inch square pan

Timing Information:

Preparation	Cooking	Total Time
10 mins	1 hr	1 hr 10 mins

Nutritional Information:

Calories	265 kcal
Carbohydrates	18.1 g
Cholesterol	111 mg
Fat	12.9 g
Fiber	2.4 g
Protein	18.7 g
Sodium	496 mg

* Percent Daily Values are based on a 2,000 calorie diet.

SIMPLE CREAM OF MEATBALL

Ingredients

- 5 pounds Italian meatballs
- 1 (10.75 oz.) can condensed cream of mushroom soup
- 3/4 C. water
- 2 C. sour cream

Directions

- Get a container and mix your sour cream, meatballs, water, and mushroom together. Place a lid on the container and place it in the fridge for 8 hrs.
- Now add everything to your slow cooker and cook for about 3 to 4 hours on medium until the meat is completely cooked.

Servings: 20 servings

Timing Information:

Preparation	Cooking	Total Time
8 hrs 5 mins	1 hr	9 hrs 5 mins

Nutritional Information:

Calories	427 kcal
Carbohydrates	8.8 g
Cholesterol	98 mg
Fat	35.4 g
Fiber	2.7 g
Protein	17.2 g
Sodium	962 mg

* Percent Daily Values are based on a 2,000 calorie diet.

POTATOES AND GARLIC

Ingredients

- 4 medium baking potatoes, scrubbed
- 2 tbsps olive oil
- 2 tsps garlic salt, or to taste
- salt and pepper to taste

Directions

- Set your oven to 375 degrees before doing anything else.
- Get a smaller bowl: add in olive oil.
- Get a 2nd smaller bowl add in: pepper, and garlic salt.
- Cover your potatoes with olive oil, by dipping, or rolling them in the bowl of oil. Then coat them with the dry seasonings.
- Cook the potatoes for 1 hr in the oven directly on the rack.
- Enjoy.

Amount per serving (4 total)

Timing Information:

Preparation	Cooking	Total Time
5 m	1 h	1 h 5 m

Nutritional Information:

Calories	225 kcal
Fat	6.9 g
Carbohydrates	37.5g
Protein	4.4 g
Cholesterol	0 mg
Sodium	919 mg

* Percent Daily Values are based on a 2,000 calorie diet.

BAKED POTATOES REMIX

Ingredients

- 2 tbsps olive oil
- 3 large sweet potatoes
- 2 pinches dried oregano
- 2 pinches salt
- 2 pinches ground black pepper

Directions

- Coat a casserole dish with olive oil. Then set your oven to 350 before doing anything else.
- Clean and remove the skin from your potatoes.
- Cut them into bit sized chunks.
- Enter the potatoes in the casserole dish and stir them so they get coated with olive oil.
- Season the potatoes with pepper, oregano, and salt.
- Cook in the oven for 1 hr.
- Enjoy.

Amount per serving (4 total)

Timing Information:

Preparation	Cooking	Total Time
10 m	1 h 5 m	1 h 15 m

Nutritional Information:

Calories	321 kcal
Fat	7.3 g
Carbohydrates	61g
Protein	4.8 g
Cholesterol	0 mg
Sodium	92 mg

* Percent Daily Values are based on a 2,000 calorie diet.

Sunbelt Classic Chicken

Ingredients

- 3 lbs chicken thighs
- 2 tbsps soy sauce
- 1/2 C. ketchup
- 1/4 C. corn syrup
- 1 pinch garlic powder

Directions

- Set your oven to 350 degrees before doing anything else.
- Get a bowl, combine: garlic powder, soy sauce, corn syrup, and ketchup.
- Clean your chicken and then place all the pieces in a casserole dish.
- Now top everything with the soy mix.
- Cook the chicken in the oven for 65 mins.
- Baste the meat at least 3 times before it finishes cooking.
- Enjoy.

Amount per serving (4 total)

Timing Information:

Preparation	10 m
Cooking	1 h
Total Time	1 h 10 m

Nutritional Information:

Calories	807 kcal
Fat	52 g
Carbohydrates	23.1g
Protein	59.9 g
Cholesterol	1286 mg
Sodium	1044 mg

* Percent Daily Values are based on a 2,000 calorie diet.

LEMONS AND OREGANO CHICKEN

Ingredients

- 7 chicken thighs
- 2 tsps dried oregano
- salt and pepper to taste
- 1/4 C. olive oil
- 1/2 lemon, juiced

Directions

- Set your oven to 450 degrees before doing anything else.
- Clean your chicken then top with pepper, salt, and oregano then layer the pieces into a casserole dish coated with nonstick spray.
- Get a bowl, combine: lemon juice and oil.
- Coat the chicken with half of the mix.
- Cook everything in the oven for 20 mins.
- Now flip the pieces and top the contents with the rest of the lemon mix.
- Cook the dish for 20 more mins in the oven.
- Enjoy.

Amount per serving (7 total)

Timing Information:

Preparation	10 m
Cooking	50 m
Total Time	1 h 10 m

Nutritional Information:

Calories	269 kcal
Fat	22.1 g
Carbohydrates	1.1g
Protein	16.4 g
Cholesterol	79 mg
Sodium	72 mg

* Percent Daily Values are based on a 2,000 calorie diet.

THE FLUFFY SANDWICH

Ingredients

- 2 tbsps peanut butter
- 2 slices bread
- 2 1/2 tbsps marshmallow cream

Directions

- Lay two pieces of bread flat on a working surface.
- Coat one piece of bread with peanut butter, and another piece with marshmallow cream.
- Now microwave the pieces of bread for 30 secs with the highest power setting.
- Form the pieces into a sandwich and enjoy with milk.

Amount per serving (1 total)

Timing Information:

Preparation	Cooking	Total Time
4 m	1 m	5 m

Nutritional Information:

Calories	373 kcal
Fat	18.1 g
Carbohydrates	43.5g
Protein	12.1 g
Cholesterol	0 mg
Sodium	502 mg

* Percent Daily Values are based on a 2,000 calorie diet.

Oregano Mozzarella Sandwich

Ingredients

- 1/4 C. unsalted butter
- 1/8 tsp garlic powder (optional)
- 12 slices white bread
- 1 tsp dried oregano
- 1 (8 oz.) package shredded mozzarella cheese
- 1 (24 oz.) jar vodka marinara sauce

Directions

- Turn on the broiler before doing anything else.
- Get a baking dish and lay half of your bread pieces in it.
- On top of each piece of bread put some mozzarella. Then top the cheese with the remaining pieces of bread.
- With a butter knife coat each sandwich with some butter. Then season the butter by applying some oregano and garlic powder.
- Broil the sandwiches for 4 mins then flip it and apply more butter, oregano, and garlic to its opposite side.

- Continue broiling the sandwich for another 4 mins.
- Enjoy with the marinara as a dip.

Servings: 6

Timing Information:

Preparation	Cooking	Total Time
8 mins	7 mins	15 mins

Nutritional Information:

Calories	394 kcal
Fat	18.3 g
Carbohydrates	42g
Protein	15 g
Cholesterol	46 mg
Sodium	1032 mg

* Percent Daily Values are based on a 2,000 calorie diet.

THE REUBEN SANDWICH

Ingredients

- 1 C. sauerkraut, drained
- 10 oz. sliced deli turkey meat
- 2 tbsps butter
- 4 slices marble rye bread
- 4 slices Swiss cheese
- 4 tbsps thousand island salad dressing, or to taste

Directions

- Place the following in a bowl: turkey, and sauerkraut.
- Place the mix in the microwave for 1 mins.
- Now coat one side of each piece of bread with butter liberally then coat the other piece with some dressing.
- Evenly distribute your Swiss, sauerkraut, and turkey on two pieces of bread.
- Top the meat with the other piece of bread with its buttered side facing upwards.

- Now fry your sandwiches with the buttered side facing downwards for 8 mins, flipping the sandwich halfway.
- Enjoy.

Amount per serving (2 total)

Timing Information:

Preparation	Cooking	Total Time
10 m	10 m	20 m

Nutritional Information:

Calories	760 kcal
Fat	43.9 g
Carbohydrates	48.9g
Protein	44.7 g
Cholesterol	150 mg
Sodium	3088 mg

* Percent Daily Values are based on a 2,000 calorie diet.

PARMIGIANO-REGGIANO SANDWICH

Ingredients

- 1/4 C. butter, softened
- 1 C. freshly grated Parmigiano-Reggiano cheese
- 8 slices cooked bacon
- 4 slices Cheddar cheese
- 8 white bread

Directions

- Get a bowl, evenly mix: parmesan, and butter.
- Get a frying hot with nonstick spray.
- Layer one piece of cheddar, and two pieces of bacon on half of your pieces of bread. Then put another piece of bread to form a sandwich. Coat sandwich with butter parmesan mix on both sides.
- Cook for 4 mins per side.
- Enjoy.

Amount per serving (4 total)

Timing Information:

Preparation	Cooking	Total Time
10 mins	6 mins	16 mins

Nutritional Information:

Calories	748 kcal
Fat	50.1 g
Carbohydrates	30.4g
Protein	43 g
Cholesterol	135 mg
Sodium	2211 mg

* Percent Daily Values are based on a 2,000 calorie diet.

Tomato and Egg Stir Fry

Ingredients

- 2 tbsps avocado oil, or as needed
- 6 eggs, beaten
- 4 ripe tomatoes, sliced into wedges
- 2 green onions, thinly sliced

Directions

- Get your frying pan hot with medium heat and 1 tbsp of avocado oil.
- Fry your eggs until done around 1 min and plate the eggs
- Add 1 more tbsp of oil in your pan and stir fry tomatoes until dry for around two mins. Now add some onions and begin to re-fry the eggs and onion for half a min.
- Enjoy.

Servings: 3 servings

Timing Information:

Preparation	Cooking	Total Time
10 mins	5 mins	15 mins

Nutritional Information:

Calories	264 kcal
Carbohydrates	9.2 g
Cholesterol	372 mg
Fat	19.7 g
Fiber	2.6 g
Protein	14.5 g
Sodium	151 mg

* Percent Daily Values are based on a 2,000 calorie diet.

CHICKEN AND ONIONS TORTILLAS

Ingredients

- 1 lb skinless, boneless chicken breast halves - cut into strips
- 1 tbsp vegetable oil
- 1 onion, sliced into strips
- 2 tbsps salsa
- 10 (10 inch) flour tortillas
- 2 C. shredded Cheddar-Monterey Jack cheese blend

Directions

- Coat a baking sheet with nonstick spray. Then set your oven to 350 degrees before anything else.
- Stir fry your chicken until fully done. Then combine in your onions and cook until they are see-through. Then add your salsa and shut off the heat.
- For 1 min in the microwave warm your tortillas.
- On one side of each tortilla layer it with cheese and chicken.
- Fold over the other side to form a quesadilla.

- Do this for all ingredients and tortillas.
- Place everything on the greased sheet and cook in the oven for until the cheese is bubbly.
- Enjoy.

Amount per serving (10 total)

Timing Information:

Preparation	Cooking	Total Time
20 m	7 m	27 m

Nutritional Information:

Calories	381 kcal
Fat	8.4 g
Carbohydrates	42.1g
Protein	21.7 g
Cholesterol	46 mg
Sodium	530 mg

* Percent Daily Values are based on a 2,000 calorie diet.

PECOS PASTA

Ingredients

- 4 oz macaroni
- 1 tbsp butter
- 1 green bell pepper, chopped
- 1 onion, chopped
- 1 (8.75 oz) can whole kernel corn, drained
- 1 (15 oz) can chili with beans
- 1 tsp salt
- 1 tsp ground black pepper

Directions

- Boil your macaroni in salt and water for 10 mins. Remove liquid excesses.
- Fry your, diced onions, and diced bell pepper in butter until onion is soft. Mix in some salt and pepper, chili beans, and corn. Lower your heating source and let everything simmer for 6 mins.

- Finally combine in your macaroni and place a lid on the pan. Simmer for another 5 mins.
- Enjoy.

Servings: 4 servings

Timing Information:

Preparation	Cooking	Total Time
10 mins	20 mins	30 mins

Nutritional Information:

Calories	315 kcal
Carbohydrates	49.2 g
Cholesterol	25 mg
Fat	9.7 g
Fiber	7.8 g
Protein	11.9 g
Sodium	1336 mg

* Percent Daily Values are based on a 2,000 calorie diet.

SWEET CREPES

Ingredients

- 4 eggs, lightly beaten
- 1 1/3 C. milk
- 2 tbsps butter, melted
- 1 C. all-purpose flour
- 2 tbsps white sugar
- 1/2 tsp salt

Directions

- In a large bowl, add all the ingredients and beat till well combined and smooth.
- Lightly, grease a crepe pan and heat on medium heat.
- Place about 3 tbsps of mixture and tilt the pan to spread it evenly.
- Cook for about 1-2 minutes per side.
- Repeat with the remaining mixture.
- Serve hot.

Amount per serving (8 total)

Timing Information:

Preparation	10 m
Cooking	10 m
Total Time	20 m

Nutritional Information:

Calories	164 kcal
Fat	7.7 g
Carbohydrates	17.2g
Protein	6.4 g
Cholesterol	111 mg
Sodium	235 mg

* Percent Daily Values are based on a 2,000 calorie diet.

CREAM CHEESE CREPES

Ingredients

- 3 ounces cream cheese, softened
- 2 eggs
- 1 tsp ground cinnamon
- 1 tbsp sugar-free syrup
- 1 tsp butter

Directions

- In a bowl, crack the eggs and beat well.
- Add the cream cheese, 1 tbsp at one time and beat till well combined.
- Add the sugar-free syrup and cinnamon and beat till smooth.
- Grease a skillet with butter and heat on medium heat and then reduce the heat to medium-low.
- Place the desired amount of the mixture and tilt the pan to spread it evenly.
- Cook for about 4 minutes and carefully, flip it.

- Cook for about 1-2 minutes.
- Repeat with the remaining mixture.
- Serve hot.

Amount per serving (2 total)

Timing Information:

Preparation	5 m
Cooking	20 m
Total Time	25 m

Nutritional Information:

Calories	241 kcal
Fat	21.8 g
Carbohydrates	2.4g
Protein	9.6 g
Cholesterol	238 mg
Sodium	215 mg

* Percent Daily Values are based on a 2,000 calorie diet.

CLASSICAL COLLEGE BURGER I

Ingredients

- 1 lb ground beef
- 1 slice bread, crumbled
- 1 egg
- 2 tbsps prepared mustard
- 3 tbsps Worcestershire sauce
- garlic salt to taste
- salt and pepper to taste

Directions

- Take out a large bowl and mix beef, egg, Worcestershire sauce and mustard.
- Now make 8 patties and also add some salt, pepper and garlic (salt according to your taste).
- Now cook these patties in a skillet that is over medium heat for about 15 mins to reach the required tenderness.

Serving: 8

Timing Information:

Preparation	Cooking	Total Time
5 mins	15 mins	20 mins

Nutritional Information:

Calories	229 kcal
Carbohydrates	3.5 g
Cholesterol	82 mg
Fat	18.2 g
Fiber	0.2 g
Protein	12.1 g
Sodium	247 mg

* Percent Daily Values are based on a 2,000 calorie diet.

Easy American Potato Salad

Ingredients

- 1 (1 oz.) package ranch dressing mix
- 2 C. mayonnaise
- 3/4 C. diced green onion
- 1 lb bacon slices
- 5 lbs unpeeled red potatoes

Directions

- For 22 mins boil your potatoes in water and salt. Then remove the liquid and chunk the potatoes when cool.
- Place the chunks in a bowl and chill them in the fridge for 3 hrs.
- Get a 2nd bowl, combine: green onions, mayo, and ranch.
- Place a covering of plastic on this bowl, and place it in the fridge as well for 3 hrs.
- For 17 mins microwave your bacon wrapped in paper towels.
- Once the bacon is cool, break it into pieces.
- Add the bacon to the mayo mix.

- Stir everything then add the mayo mix to the bowl with the potatoes.
- Stir everything again, then serve.
- Enjoy.

Amount per serving (16 total)

Timing Information:

Preparation	30 m
Cooking	30 m
Total Time	1 h

Nutritional Information:

Calories	353 kcal
Fat	25.9 g
Carbohydrates	24.8g
Protein	6.5 g
Cholesterol	21 mg
Sodium	503 mg

* Percent Daily Values are based on a 2,000 calorie diet.

CHICKEN PARMIGIANA

Ingredients

- 1 egg, beaten
- 2 oz. dry bread crumbs
- 2 skinless, boneless chicken breast halves
- 3/4 (16 oz.) jar spaghetti sauce
- 2 oz. shredded mozzarella cheese
- 1/4 C. grated Parmesan cheese

Directions

- Coat a cookie sheet with oil then set your oven to 350 degrees before doing anything else.
- Get a bowl and add in your eggs.
- Get a 2nd bowl and add in your bread crumbs.
- Coat your chicken first with the eggs then with the bread crumbs.
- Lay your pieces of chicken on the cookie sheet and cook them in the oven for 45 mins, until they are fully done.

- Now add half of your pasta sauce to a casserole dish and lay in your chicken on top of the sauce.
- Place the rest of the sauce on top of the chicken pieces. Then add a topping of parmesan and mozzarella over everything.
- Cook the parmigiana in the oven for 25 mins.
- Enjoy.

Amount per serving (2 total)

Timing Information:

Preparation	30 m
Cooking	1 h
Total Time	1 h 30 m

Nutritional Information:

Calories	528 kcal
Fat	18.3 g
Carbohydrates	44.9g
Protein	43.5 g
Cholesterol	184 mg
Sodium	1309 mg

* Percent Daily Values are based on a 2,000 calorie diet.

UPSTATE NEW YORK CHICKEN

Ingredients

- 2 tbsps olive oil
- 2 cloves garlic, minced
- 1 tbsp chopped fresh rosemary
- salt and ground black pepper to taste
- 6 skinless, boneless chicken breast halves
- 1 (8 oz.) package cream cheese, softened
- 1 (10.5 oz.) can cream of mushroom soup
- 1 C. white wine

Directions

- Set your oven to 350 degrees before doing anything else.
- Begin to stir fry your garlic for 5 mins in olive oil then add in the pepper, salt, and rosemary.
- Stir in your chicken and cook the meat for 7 mins each side, then place everything into a casserole dish.

- Get a bowl, combine: white wine, cream cheese, and mushroom soup. Then top the chicken with the mix once it is smooth.
- Cook everything in the oven for 1 hr.
- Enjoy.

Amount per serving (6 total)

Timing Information:

Preparation	15 m
Cooking	50 m
Total Time	1 h 5 m

Nutritional Information:

Calories	363 kcal
Fat	22.8 g
Carbohydrates	5.8g
Protein	25.7 g
Cholesterol	100 mg
Sodium	481 mg

* Percent Daily Values are based on a 2,000 calorie diet.

CORN AND BEEF TACOS

Ingredients

- 2 lbs ground beef
- 1 onion, chopped
- 2 (15 oz.) cans ranch-style beans
- 1 (15.25 oz.) can whole kernel corn
- 1 (10 oz.) can diced tomatoes with green chile peppers
- 1 (14.5 oz.) can peeled and diced tomatoes with juice
- 1 (1.25 oz.) package taco seasoning mix

Directions

- Cook your onions and beef for 10 mins then remove oil excesses.
- Combine with the beef your chili peppers, beans, taco seasoning, tomatoes, and corn. Stir the contents for a min. Cook over medium heat for 17 mins.
- Enjoy.

Amount per serving (8 total)

Timing Information:

Preparation	Cooking	Total Time
15 m	30 m	45 m

Nutritional Information:

Calories	520 kcal
Fat	30.7 g
Carbohydrates	32.6g
Protein	26.7 g
Cholesterol	96 mg
Sodium	1289 mg

* Percent Daily Values are based on a 2,000 calorie diet.

Keema

(Asian Inspired Ground Beef)

Ingredients

- 2 tbsps butter, or more to taste
- 2 onions, diced
- 1 clove garlic, minced
- 1 1/2 tbsps curry powder
- 2 1/2 tsps salt
- 1 tsp ground turmeric
- 1 tsp cayenne pepper

- 1/2 tsp ground black pepper
- 1/4 tsp ground ginger
- 1/2 cinnamon stick
- 1 lb ground beef
- 2 potatoes, diced
- 2 tomatoes, diced

Directions

- Cook onions and garlic in hot butter for about 5 minutes or until tender.
- Add ground beef into the pan and cook this until you see that it is brown before adding a mixture of curry powder, black pepper, salt, turmeric, cayenne pepper, ginger, and cinnamon into the pan.

- Now stir in some potatoes and tomatoes, and cook this after turning the heat down to medium for about 20 minutes to get the potatoes tender.
- Serve.

Serving: 6

Timing Information:

Preparation	Cooking	Total Time
15 mins	30 mins	45 mins

Nutritional Information:

Calories	280 kcal
Carbohydrates	19.2 g
Cholesterol	57 mg
Fat	16.1 g
Fiber	3.5 g
Protein	15 g
Sodium	1049 mg

* Percent Daily Values are based on a 2,000 calorie diet.

CREAMY GROUND BEEF

Ingredients

- 1 lb ground beef
- 1/4 cup all-purpose flour
- 1 cube beef bouillon
- 3/4 tsp salt
- 1 pinch ground black pepper
- 2 1/4 cups milk
- 1/4 tsp Worcestershire sauce

Directions

- Cook beef over medium heat for about 7 minutes or until brown before adding pepper, flour, salt and bouillon, and cook all this for five minutes.
- Now add milk and Worcestershire sauce slowly into the pan before cooking all this for 10 minutes.
- Serve.

Serving: 8

Timing Information:

Preparation	Cooking	Total Time
10 mins	20 mins	30 mins

Nutritional Information:

Calories	201 kcal
Carbohydrates	8.5 g
Cholesterol	53 mg
Fat	10.8 g
Fiber	0.2 g
Protein	16.3 g
Sodium	518 mg

* Percent Daily Values are based on a 2,000 calorie diet.

Delicious Ground Beef and Tomatoes

Ingredients

- 1 lb ground beef
- 2 (29 ounce) cans tomato sauce
- 3 tbsps dried basil
- 3 tbsps dried oregano
- 3 tbsps onion powder
- 2 tbsps garlic powder
- 2 tbsps white sugar
- 1 tsp salt
- 1/2 tsp ground black pepper

Directions

- Cook beef over medium heat for about 7 minutes or until brown before adding tomato sauce, garlic powder, basil, oregano, sugar, salt, onion powder and pepper.
- Now turn down the heat to low and cook for one full hour until you see that the sauce is thick.

Serving: 8

Timing Information:

Preparation	Cooking	Total Time
10 mins	1 hr 15 mins	1 hr 25 mins

Nutritional Information:

Calories	187 kcal
Carbohydrates	19.2 g
Cholesterol	35 mg
Fat	7.4 g
Fiber	4.3 g
Protein	13.3 g
Sodium	1390 mg

* Percent Daily Values are based on a 2,000 calorie diet.

GROUND BEEF FESTIVAL

Ingredients

- 1 lb ground beef
- 1 tbsp garlic pepper seasoning
- 1 (15 ounce) can corn, drained
- 1 cup ranch dressing
- 1 cup salsa
- 1 tbsp dried oregano
- shredded Cheddar cheese, or more to taste
- 2 cups cooked rice, or to taste(optional)

Directions

- Cook beef and garlic over medium heat for about 7 minutes or until brown before adding corn, oregano, ranch dressing and salsa.
- Cook all this for 10 minutes.
- Pour this over rice for serving.

Serving: 4

Timing Information:

Preparation	Cooking	Total Time
10 mins	15 mins	25 mins

Nutritional Information:

Calories	815 kcal
Carbohydrates	50 g
Cholesterol	104 mg
Fat	56 g
Fiber	4.1 g
Protein	29.9 g
Sodium	1795 mg

* Percent Daily Values are based on a 2,000 calorie diet.

THE EASIEST BEEF CHILI

Ingredients

- 1 lb ground beef
- 1 large onion, diced
- 1 (15 ounce) can ranch-style beans
- 1 (10 ounce) can diced tomatoes with green chili peppers
- 1 (1.25 ounce) package chili seasoning mix
- salt and pepper to taste
- 2 tsps chili powder, or to taste
- 1 cup water, or as needed

Directions

- Cook beef and onion until brown before adding beans, chili powder, diced tomatoes, pepper, chili seasoning, salt and water.
- Turn down the heat to low and cook for two full hours.

Serving: 4

Timing Information:

Preparation	Cooking	Total Time
10 mins	2 hr	2 hr 10 mins

Nutritional Information:

Calories	382 kcal
Carbohydrates	26.8 g
Cholesterol	70 mg
Fat	18.7 g
Fiber	8.4 g
Protein	27 g
Sodium	1701 mg

* Percent Daily Values are based on a 2,000 calorie diet.

PEPPERS AND ONIONS BROWN RICE

Ingredients

- 2 C. water
- 1 C. brown rice
- 1/2 red bell peppers, seeded and chopped
- 1/4 red onion, chopped
- 1 C. shredded low-fat Cheddar cheese

Directions

- Get your water and rice boiling before placing a lid on the pot, setting the heat to low, and letting the contents cook for 47 mins.
- Stir fry your onions and peppers in nonstick spray, until brown, and combine them with the rice, when it is finished.
- Combine in your cheese and let it melt before plating the dish.
- Enjoy.

Amount per serving (8 total)

Timing Information:

Preparation	10 m
Cooking	45 m
Total Time	55 m

Nutritional Information:

Calories	95 kcal
Fat	1.5 g
Carbohydrates	15g
Protein	4.9 g
Cholesterol	3 mg
Sodium	87 mg

* Percent Daily Values are based on a 2,000 calorie diet.

OATMEAL FOR BREAKFAST

Ingredients

- 1 egg, beaten
- 1 3/4 C. milk
- 1/2 C. packed brown sugar
- 1 C. rolled oats
- 2 tbsps butter

Directions

- Get a big pot and pour in your milk then add: brown sugar and beaten eggs.
- Get everything boiling and continually stir the mix for about 4 mins.
- Shut off the heat and then add your butter.
- Let the butter melt.
- Enjoy warm.

Amount per serving (3 total)

Timing Information:

Preparation	Cooking	Total Time
5 m	10 m	15 m

Nutritional Information:

Calories	357 kcal
Fat	13.9 g
Carbohydrates	48.8g
Protein	10.5 g
Cholesterol	94 mg
Sodium	145 mg

* Percent Daily Values are based on a 2,000 calorie diet.

QUICK EGG FRITTATA

Ingredients

- 2 large eggs
- salt
- fresh ground pepper

- 2 tbsps shredded cheese
- 2/3 C. vegetables
- 2 tbsps fresh herbs

Directions

- Set your oven to 350 degrees before doing anything else.
- Get a bowl, combine: herbs, cheese, and eggs.
- Coat a skillet with nonstick spray then add in your veggies.
- Cook the veggies for 1 min then add in the egg mix.
- Set the heat to low and let the bottom of the eggs set with a lid on the pan for 10 mins.
- Now place the frittata in the oven for 5 to 10 more mins until the top is set.
- Enjoy.

Amount per serving: 1

Timing Information:

Preparation	5 mins
Total Time	25 mins

Nutritional Information:

Calories	239.0 kcal
Cholesterol	440.7mg
Sodium	408.4mg
Carbohydrates	3.0g
Protein	18.0g

* Percent Daily Values are based on a 2,000 calorie diet.

Disco Fries

(Fries with Mozzarella and Gravy)

Remember if you do not feel like frying potatoes. Just buy some frozen fries and roast them in the oven for about 20 then top everything with the cheese and some hot gravy.

Ingredients

- 1 quart vegetable oil for frying
- 1 (10.25 oz.) can beef gravy
- 5 medium potatoes, cut into fries
- 2 C. mozzarella

Directions

- Deep fry your fries in oil while heating your gravy.
- Cook the fries for about 6 mins.
- Place the fries on some paper towel to remove the excess oils.
- Now top the fries with the cheese.

- Add the hot gravy over the cheese and let it melt from the heat.
- Enjoy hot.

Amount per serving (4 total)

Timing Information:

Preparation	5 m
Cooking	20 m
Total Time	25 m

Nutritional Information:

Calories	708 kcal
Fat	46.3 g
Carbohydrates	51g
Protein	23.8 g
Cholesterol	78 mg
Sodium	773 mg

* Percent Daily Values are based on a 2,000 calorie diet.

ITALIAN STYLE EGGS

Ingredients

- 2 tbsps extra virgin olive oil
- 4 ripe tomatoes, chopped
- 4 eggs
- salt and pepper to taste

Directions

- For 6 mins cook your tomatoes in hot oil. Simply break the eggs into the tomatoes and add some pepper and salt. Fry until you reach the firmness that you enjoy the most.

Amount per serving (4 total)

Timing Information:

Preparation	Cooking	Total Time
5 m	10 m	15 m

Nutritional Information:

Calories	154 kcal
Fat	11.9 g
Carbohydrates	5.3g
Protein	7.5 g
Cholesterol	186 mg
Sodium	374 mg

* Percent Daily Values are based on a 2,000 calorie diet.

NUTELLA ROLL UP

Ingredients
- 1 tortilla
- 1/4 cup chocolate-hazelnut spread (such as Nutella)
- 1 small banana

Directions
- Put chocolate spread on the corners of a tortilla that is warmed in the microwave oven for 10 seconds and fold it around the banana slice.
- Cut it into half and serve.

Servings: 2

Timing Information:

Preparation	Cooking	Total Time
5 mins		5 mins

Nutritional Information:

Calories	317 kcal
Carbohydrates	49g
Cholesterol	0 mg
Fat	11.9 g
Protein	5.5 g
Sodium	259 mg

* Percent Daily Values are based on a 2,000 calorie diet.

MICROWAVE NUTELLA CAKE

Ingredients
- 1/4 cup self-rising flour
- 1/4 cup white sugar
- 1 egg
- 3 tbsps vegetable oil
- 3 tbsps milk
- 2 tbsps unsweetened cocoa powder, or more to taste
- 2 tbsps chocolate-hazelnut spread (such as Nutella), or more to taste
- 1/2 tsp salt
- 1/2 tsp vanilla extract

Directions
- Put all the ingredients mentioned into a large sized mug and whisk it until smooth.
- Now cook this in a microwave oven for about 2 minutes or until the cake has risen.
- Serve.

Servings: 2

Timing Information:

Preparation	Cooking	Total Time
10 mins	5 mins	15 mins

Nutritional Information:

Calories	475 kcal
Carbohydrates	50.4g
Cholesterol	95 mg
Fat	28.8 g
Protein	7.5 g
Sodium	840 mg

* Percent Daily Values are based on a 2,000 calorie diet.

A HIPSTER'S FAVORITE COFFEE

Ingredients
- 2 cups ice cubes
- 1 1/2 cups milk
- 3 tbsps white sugar
- 2 tbsps chocolate-hazelnut spread (such as Nutella)
- 4 tsps instant coffee granules
- 1 tbsp vanilla extract

Directions
- Put all the ingredients mentioned into a blender and blend for about 30 seconds or until the required smoothness is achieved.
- Enjoy your unique tasting coffee.

Servings: 2

Timing Information:

Preparation	Cooking	Total Time
10 mins		10 mins

Nutritional Information:

Calories	267 kcal
Carbohydrates	38.3g
Cholesterol	15 mg
Fat	8.1 g
Protein	7.3 g
Sodium	99 mg

* Percent Daily Values are based on a 2,000 calorie diet.

TACO LOCAL

Ingredients

- 1 1/4 lbs ground beef
- 1/2 onion, chopped
- 1 (1.25 oz.) package dry taco seasoning mix
- 3/4 C. water
- 1 (14 oz.) can refried beans
- 4 oz. process cheese food (such as Velveeta(R)), cut into small cubes
- 10 (6 inch) flour tortillas, warmed
- 10 crisp taco shells, warmed

Directions

- For 11 mins fry your onions and beef. Then remove any excess oils.
- Get a saucepan and add water and taco seasoning.
- Get this mixture boiling.
- Once boiling lower the heat and let it simmer for 12 mins.

- After 12 mins combine the taco seasoning mix with the beef and let the contents continue to lightly boil.
- Get a 2nd saucepan and mix cubed cheese and refried beans together. Heat for 10 mins stir and heat for 12 more mins.
- Layer each tortilla with an equal amount of refried beans and cheese. Fold each tortilla around a taco.
- Then add in your seasoned ground beef.

Amount per serving (10 total)

Timing Information:

Preparation	Cooking	Total Time
10 m	20 m	30 m

Nutritional Information:

Calories	347 kcal
Fat	16 g
Carbohydrates	31.9g
Protein	17.5 g
Cholesterol	49 mg
Sodium	801 mg

* Percent Daily Values are based on a 2,000 calorie diet.

Spaghetti Taco

Ingredients

- 1 (16 oz.) package angel hair pasta
- 1 (28 oz.) jar spaghetti sauce
- 1 (5.8 oz.) package crisp taco shells
- 1/4 C. grated Parmesan cheese

Directions

- Cook your angel hair in boiling water and salt for 6 mins until al dente.
- Remove all liquid from the pot.
- Put the pasta back in the pot with sauce and heat everything back up.
- Warm your taco shells for 1 min in the microwave.
- Add pasta to the tacos and garnish with 1 tsp of parmesan.
- Enjoy.

Amount per serving (12 total)

Timing Information:

Preparation	Cooking	Total Time
5 m	15 m	20 m

Nutritional Information:

Calories	236 kcal
Fat	6.2 g
Carbohydrates	38.5g
Protein	6.8 g
Cholesterol	3 mg
Sodium	425 mg

* Percent Daily Values are based on a 2,000 calorie diet.

AUTHENTIC TOMATO SAUCE

Use this sauce a topping for any type of pasta. Remember, to make pasta get your water boiling in a big pot. Then once it is boiling, add your pasta to the water and let it boil for 9 minutes.

Ingredients

- 2 tbsp olive oil
- 6 garlic cloves (minced)
- 2 tsp chili flakes, optional
- 1 (28 oz.) cans crushed tomatoes
- 1/2 C. water
- 1/4 C. fresh basil (chopped)
- 1 tsp salt

Directions

- In a frying pan, cook the oil, chili flakes and garlic on medium-high heat till just aromatic.
- Stir in the tomatoes, 1/2 of the basil and salt and bring to a boil.
- Add the water and reduce the heat, then simmer for about 1 hour.
- Serve with a garnishing of the remaining basil alongside the pasta of your choice.

Amount per serving: 4

Timing Information:

Preparation	10 mins
Total Time	1 hr 40 mins

Nutritional Information:

Calories	122.1
Fat	7.3g
Cholesterol	0.0mg
Sodium	1021.4mg
Carbohydrates	14.6g
Protein	2.0g

* Percent Daily Values are based on a 2,000 calorie diet.

A SIMPLE QUICHE FOR COLLEGE

Ingredients

- 1 tbsp butter
- 1 large onion, diced
- 3 eggs
- 1/3 cup heavy cream
- 1/3 cup shredded Swiss cheese
- 1 (9 inch pie) unbaked pie crust

Directions

- Preheat your oven to 375 degrees F and put some oil over the quiche dish.
- Melt butter over medium heat and then cook onions in it until soft.
- Now whisk eggs and cream together in a bowl and then add cheese.
- Place onion at the bottom of the dish and pour this mixture over it.
- Bake in the preheated oven for about 30 minutes or until the top of the quiche is golden brown in color.

Serving: 8

Timing Information:

Preparation	Cooking	Total Time
10 mins	30 mins	40 mins

Nutritional Information:

Calories	212 kcal
Carbohydrates	12.7 g
Cholesterol	91 mg
Fat	15.7 g
Fiber	1.1 g
Protein	5.4 g
Sodium	211 mg

* Percent Daily Values are based on a 2,000 calorie diet.

CHICKEN CUTLETS

Ingredients

- 4 skinless, boneless chicken breast halves - pounded to 1/2 inch thickness
- 2 tbsps all-purpose flour
- 1 egg, beaten
- 1 cup panko bread crumbs
- 1 cup oil for frying, or as needed

Directions

- Get three bowls. Bowl 1 for chicken. Bowl 2 for bread crumbs. Bowl 3 for eggs.
- Cover chicken with flour first. Then with egg, and finally with crumbs.
- Get a frying pan and heat 1/4 inch of oil. Fry your chicken for 5 mins on each side.
- Remove excess oil.
- Enjoy.

Servings: 4 servings

Timing Information:

Preparation	Cooking	Total Time
10 mins	10 mins	20 mins

Nutritional Information:

Calories	297 kcal
Carbohydrates	22.2 g
Cholesterol	118 mg
Fat	11.4 g
Fiber	0.1 g
Protein	31.2 g
Sodium	251 mg

* Percent Daily Values are based on a 2,000 calorie diet.

SIMPLY BAKED BROCCOLI

Ingredients

- 1 (12 oz.) bag broccoli florets
- 1/2 red onion, sliced
- 8 fresh sage leaves, torn
- 2 tbsps extra-virgin olive oil
- 1/2 tsp salt
- 1/2 tsp garlic salt
- 1/4 tsp ground black pepper

Directions

- Cover a casserole dish or sheet for baking with foil and then set your oven to 400 degrees before doing anything else.
- Layer your broccoli evenly throughout the dish and top with sage leaves and onions. Garnish all the veggies with olive oil and then black pepper, regular salt, and garlic salt.
- Cook the veggies in the oven for 27 mins until slightly browned and crunchy.
- Enjoy.

Amount per serving (4 total)

Timing Information:

Preparation	Cooking	Total Time
10 m	20 m	30 m

Nutritional Information:

Calories	97 kcal
Fat	7.1 g
Carbohydrates	7.3g
Protein	2.6 g
Cholesterol	0 mg
Sodium	546 mg

* Percent Daily Values are based on a 2,000 calorie diet.

THANKS FOR READING! JOIN THE CLUB AND KEEP ON COOKING WITH 6 MORE COOKBOOKS....

http://bit.ly/1TdrStv

 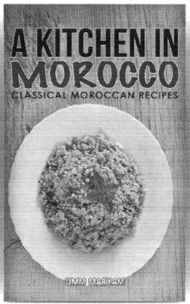 

To grab the box sets simply follow the link mentioned above, or tap one of book covers.

This will take you to a page where you can simply enter your email address and a PDF version of the box sets will be emailed to you.

Hope you are ready for some serious cooking!

http://bit.ly/1TdrStv

COME ON...
LET'S BE FRIENDS :)

We adore our readers and love connecting with them socially.

Like BookSumo on Facebook and let's get social!

Facebook

And also check out the BookSumo Cooking Blog.

Food Lover Blog

Made in the USA
Lexington, KY
28 November 2016